conversation with grief

poems and prose

TETYANA DENFORD

TBD
Books

First Printing: 2021
Copyright @2021 by Tetyana Denford
TBD Books
Cover design: Emir Orucevic

Tetyana Denford
Tetyana.Denford@gmail.com
New York, NY
www.tetyanadenford.com
www.instagram.com/tetyanawrites

Also by Tetyana Denford:

Motherland

Other 'conversation books' in this series:

conversation with motherhood

conversation with love

This book is dedicated to those
who have lost love—

the weight of grief will always
help you find it again.

ACKNOWLEDGEMENTS

To the people in my life who constantly show me love
and patience and guidance, and who remind me that
sometimes endings are beautiful beginnings.

And to my husband and children, I write my stories for
you, so that one day you can reach for me
when I'm not here anymore.

The grace with which we embrace life,
in spite of the pain, the sorrows,
is always a measure of what has gone before.

-Alice Walker

PREFACE

n March 2020, I published my first novel, *Motherland.* As
t was a story based on an epic event in my
grandmother's life, the book was a bit of atonement for
he woman who had lived a hard 95 years. I remember
howing her the book, I remember kissing her on her soft
heek, I remember how she looked at me when I smiled
t her.

A month later, she died.

was unhooked from my life. I was floating, but heavy; I
elt mortality like a full sentence written in magical text.
The world felt surreal, and yet profoundly real.

didn't want to read, I did a lot of crying, watched too
much television, and I listened to songs that reminded
me of her. I thought I'd try and write, but no words
ame. I sat at my laptop, staring at blank pages, looking
or 'signs' of her out my window. I think I slept, I'm not
ure I did, and I definitely didn't dream. My mind kept
ravelling in restless circles looking for answers, and
oming up empty. As I was figuring out how to heal, I
vas also having conversations with people (some
trangers, some friends) about grief and what it means to
hem, how they feel it, how they carry it, and how it

changes them and connects them to a deeper purpose. I also started thinking about how important it is to have conversations in general: small bursts of time where we have the mental capacity to think, feel, listen, and grow. Conversations about grief, but also where grief lives, too: in hope, in motherhood, in life, self, childhood, and love. These conversations made it feel like I had a friend with me, for a moment in time. It's kind of like an invisible thread, connecting all of us.

And suddenly, I started to write again. Part of it was because I felt a kinship: I was now part of a group of hearts that were bruised by circumstance a bit more than others. Grief, I learned, does that— it brings the pieces of humanity together. It teaches us how to adjust, how to wallow, how to appreciate what we've been given, even if the cards we've been handed are pretty rough. Part of my writing was definitely because I wanted to talk, or imagine talking to people, about the things we all go through but don't share very often on a deeper level. So many of us think we don't have the time to indulge in little stories about our lives, and yet, we do every day, in little ways. By talking.

Six months into writing this book, I saw my neighbor, Linda, and I told her how I felt. 'I lost someone important to me too,' she said to me, and smiled. 'We all do. Maybe that's life reminding us about love— how to feel it, and how to hope for it again. Talking about it is what we can do for each other.' And it was then that I realized I wanted to write a series of books that were

onnected by conversation, comforting little books that
ve could keep in our pockets, stories to make us feel less
lone and to see us through our journeys. So, this was
he first book in a series of comforting, pocket-sized
houghts and stories— like taking a walk with a friend.

o, here's to the talking, the remembering. Here's to
loing what we need in order to feel connected when the
vorld feels confusing.

Here's to conversation.

kintsugi

you have to look at the broken pieces
closely.
Make time for them.
Even use a magnifying glass if you have to.
You can't carry anything else in there,
they are kind of useless for what they used to be.
Pay attention. Healing needs focus.
They sit in your palms and wait for you
to find gold, from somewhere, anywhere,
and pour it onto the edges like hard honey
(remember that the edges don't disappear,
ever, the edges will always be there)
and you cover them all with thick rivers,
estuaries of mended paths
revealing new ways the broken shards have travelled
and your hands wait patiently, still empty,
holding something that was broken.
Watching it heal.
Your eyes will always find what broke,
and you'll follow it,
you'll follow the edges of what you broke
and what they broke
and what we broke
and you wait until
your hot palms can carry what you loved again
safely
never as it was
but as it will be.

love (loss) language

Grief has a love language: consistency. Promise.
We live with grief, deaths of a kind—
we grieve our children getting older and
our parents dying, we grieve the lives we led
before illness and tragedy, we spent tender years
longing for the death
of our carefree former selves
and then we mourn the uncertainty of adulthood
and responsibility.
We grieve friendships ending,
lost first loves and first kisses, we grieve the last time
we carried our babies and the first time we promised
to love someone forever.
We bury our old dreams and then unbury them
with hands that are wiser and older but then we cry
when we see that those stories corroded and changed
and changed shape in the dark that we'd left them in,
so we buy roses to make the change seem hopeful.
We still hope, that's what grief teaches us.
We keep digging and planting and tearing things
from their roots
to see progress.
We watch the world change and falter and break
and disappear
and we wait for the new book to buy
and the new dress to wear
and we step our feet out the door.

We grieve every day
so we have something new
to live for.

I didn't think it felt right
for her once feeling body,
the warm-blooded weight of her,
to be sleeping in stone.
It was unfair that she would be so cold.
What would she think of me,
her skin no longer
underneath my fingers,
her hair no longer brushed
by my hands.

What would she think of me,
that I left all of her in the dark?
Would she know the sound of my footsteps leaving?
Could she feel the doughy mark of my heels
In the ground above her head?
Or would the salt of my tears leave a mark,
feed the dying flowers,
crystallize on the granite.

Will she remember
that I was there?
The thing is, maybe the world is made like this:
of salt, and stone, and tangled hearts, and broken bones.

what it meant

She used to chase me around the house
with a wooden spoon.
Typical immigrant childhood, really.
She raised me with a disregard for tears and sympathy.
'Why the tears,' she would ask me when I felt lonely.
'I'm sad,' was my reply.
'Sad for what? You have food and a bed. Be happy.'
I tried to be
when she sprinkled grapes into my tin lunchbox
And sent me to school.
They were bruised by the afternoon.
I knew the feeling.
I tried to be happy
When she read my diary in high school,
Calling me a 'loose girl' for kissing boys.
I tried to be happy
When I saw her, frail and bird-like,
Pinching my cheeks and stroking my hair,
Telling me she loved me, really. Even so.
I'm trying to be happy,
In the days after her death
Thinking back to wooden spoons, avoidance,
shame and bruises.

blood and cherries

I remember
She would stain her lips
With beetroot and cherries,
Never asking for beauty to be carved out
In magazines or shop windows,
Of course she was taught that later
By men buying her worth,
But she would teach me
To take my fingers and squeeze fruit
Between my fingers
Until it bled.
She taught me to crush fruit
To my lips
And let the color drip onto my cracked skin
And when I smiled, my teeth were stained
As if I'd eaten someone's heart.

She and I,
used to sit in the living room
and watch soap operas
when I came home from school.
She never sat with me,
always opposite me,
and I watched her from my perch
on the green sofa that always made a mark
on my bare calves that were folded under me.
I don't remember what we watched,
because I was always watching
how her grey hair was tucked behind her ear,
or how her gold wedding band had flour stuck to it,
or how she would still be wearing her apron from the
morning.
Her feet were always bare,
and her blue veins were like maps that I'd trace
with my fingers.
Maps of my childhood.
Those are my memories.
The afternoon soap operas were my favorite,
I don't remember them much,
they don't give you maps to remember,
they give you maps to find a new way to forget
where you used to be.

diary

All I wanted was space
to write down a map of who I was.
She wanted to find me, too.
So she read my words.
Boys, she said. *Not good.*
(They were only innocent ideas of love)
You, she said. *Not good.*
(I knew it)
All I wanted was for her to give me
What she'd always wanted for herself—
A life without guilt.
A life without asking myself
Whether someone else had better answers.
The world, she said. *Not good.*
I would never know that, would I,
Unless I could have my words back.
Please, I said. *My words are good.*
But they were already broken
when she handed them back to me.
She'd seen the road,
littered with discarded ideas,
and she gave me the gift of shame
(she'd carried hers safely).

That night,
I walked into the garden
and took my place,
glittering beneath the stars.

Your words came so far, you said.
But I held my diary
and burned it.
I was both the fire and the ashes,
as the flames sighed them all into the willow tree.
And I was free.

navigating

She told me once
that it was a struggle every single day
to find herself.
I asked why, and she told me that she fought
for so long
to lose all trace of who she was.
Does war do that, I asked.
No, she responded.
I let others walk on the map
of the bones I'd buried
To find their own way to themselves.
She would never know
what she did for me and my daughters
by digging up her own bones.
I've decided I'm tired of my light being borrowed
Just so others can see better.
I want to find myself in those darkest corners,
so that my daughters can see
women waiting to be revealed.

because my one precious life was a lie

Mary Oliver told me
that I have to be able to do three things in this world.
Those are three things too little.
I loved something mortal
and it broke my heart.
I held it to my bones,
and it faded into gossamer.
I let it go, and the core of my body
collapsed like wet concrete.
So, where is the learning, Mary?
When does my grief create a better version of me?
Or do I sit in the stillness,
and wait for each breath to become
less painful than the last?
I held her to my bones;
her bird-like frame folding in on itself at the end.
I held her, Mary.
And she was the one to let go.

stitches

Save no time, whatever that old rhyme is, of nine—
but maybe, it keeps the heartache laced together and
fresh,
a tender reminder of what you risked,
a hole in your center,
burnt black and hard at the edges,
but the wind still sweeps through it,
cold like a needle.
Grief flies in, whistling,
and with every.
painful.
tug.
stitches it up tightly,
oh sometimes too tightly.
So tight that I saw you yesterday
or even this morning, I pulled the thread to pull you
closer,
Every second was four months ago.
My arms this morning were heavy with you, surely,
and not your picture,
But this morning was February.
Last Monday was this evening,
tomorrow is three weeks away,
and Death has no space for accountability.
Stitched close, the thread never ends, it is so long,
And we pull at it still, and wonder
where the time has gone.

there

How you held me
wasn't an accident.
You were there,
your arms trapping me at the waist,
pinching the meat of my cheeks,
like you wanted to take a piece for yourself.
You wanted the idea of me,
but not my purpose;
my wild was too wild for you.
But, you were there
shaking a fist at my voice
(too loud)
palming my back at church
(stand straight)
squeezing my hand as I walked to the schoolbus
(don't cry)
you were there
only a little bit reluctantly
as I walked into the house
through a cloud of onions and oil
and the flour dusted my face
as you grabbed me and kissed me as if I would
disappear.
You raised me as if
an intentional mistake;
you wanted me there
so you could catch me,
so you could feel your own strength.

dead bodies

I buried my first self at 8,
I suffocated her when they told me my accent was too
thick.
I buried my second self at 15,
I burned her when they told me the hair on my legs was
ugly.
I buried my third self at 18,
I cut her into pieces when they told me I needed to lose
weight
to gain a lover.
I buried my fourth self at 25,
I starved her when they told me I was insignificant.
I buried my fifth self at 33,
I left her behind when I gave birth to new versions of
myself.

and then I asked her

I stand in the kitchen, heat and oil
sinking into my skin like memories
imprinting for future joy and pain.

I stand next to you,
parchment skin and cotton rags
inches from my fingertips, but still too far for me to
grasp.

I watch you, the flour dust
a silhouette settling on the floor around us,
your elbows move out as your arms push
back and forth, kneading. needing.

I always wondered if you saw me,
small and quiet,
at your side.

I always wondered if you heard me ask you
how to move, how to make, how to give, how to take.

I asked you, sometimes.
And sometimes, you turned to me
when the light was soft
and the sun was setting,

and your answer
was the heat of a memory, imprinted.

what do you see

Remember what I told you,
so long ago, back when
the world felt pushed to the seams with joy.
Remember, I told you to keep my memories
not as pictures, but as feelings;
the warmth of them
many days and nights
anointing you with isolation and wonder
nights and hours, in one room.

Such a small thing, the biggest thing,
drifting in and out
of emptiness and color,
joy somehow lying prostrate
as you step around it.

Don't avoid me, because I will always know
when you leave,
your shadow ascending with your grief.
I will see you, and remind you to stay.

worship

I wasn't happy with you
For so much of my life.

You read my diary.
You told my secrets.
You exposed my light.

And yet, here I am
kneeling in the dirt
staring at a granite slab,
begging you to come back to me.

Maybe perfection isn't
what I suspect it is.

Maybe it's filth and sweat,
anger and tension.
Maybe a perfect life
Is as (im)perfect as we need
So that reality hits differently.

Maybe heroes are just
human beings that tried harder

in just one moment
that was witnessed by more than themselves.
And then they went back
to crying.

ghosts

look at you,
walking so freely in the world
like a breeze waiting to settle.
passive resentment,
a shadow across the sun.

broken mirrors

you look like me you said once
my hair on you
makes me search for mirrors
and remember my past
but you cut yours and I never did
but you did when you died
you cut that part from me forever
am I still you, then?

acronyms

demanding ends all true heroes
damning evidence always tames hatred
done everything and then hoped
darling eat all the hearts
dulling eviscerates angels then harms
don't ever ask to heal
devour enemies and the holy
determined envy animates tender heathens
demons explode ashes to hell
daisies elegantly align to heaven

away

where have you gone,
I ask when I search rooms
seeing shadows fall where you used to stand
every afternoon, 2:15 was the time,
I would be there, at your door
whispering hope under my breath
to bring you back to life,
the life that I'd had with you

no life,
at all.

in the beginning

The road softened
in the rain,
underneath my feet
it was morning
but it could have been any time of day.
I knew it was morning because
I had that naïve hope that the minutes would unfold
with magic; that feeling that children always have
And adults rarely do, apart from those first 15 minutes of
every day.

please

Carry me, when you go.
Sing a bit more.
Sign your name on that receipt, fold it flat.
I wish I'd asked her that
just to see her reaction when I did.
Impossible, she'd say.
Is it, though?
I carry you with me every single day,
so that you're not gone
but only in the next room
or a song away.
It's not impossible.
Carry me, when you go.
I carry your words,
your stories,
your smile,
the way you twist your ring on your knotted finger
round and round when you're thinking.
I carry those moments
like coins rattling in my purse,
waiting to be used up
when I feel particularly lonely or bored.
But maybe you aren't lonely now,
so you don't need to carry me anymore.
Maybe you're unburdened, finally,
and don't need the added weight of love.
I can carry that for you now.

not like this in the movies

Swells of music don't erupt,
the bells don't toll mournfully.
The clocks don't stop,
the dog doesn't languish,
the grey clouds don't part to reveal
a crisp yellow sun.
When it's done,
it's done.
It's quiet. It's stillness.
The mourners don't come.

empty rooms

All I want is to walk through rooms of love
with you.
Is that too much to ask?
Yes, she replied.
For even the biggest rooms can't hold my love anymore.
They are much too small.

our days together

Every day at 2:15,
I saw her there,
the metal of her chair like a light
underneath her milky skin
the way her eyes follow me as if
wishing she were where I was.
Or maybe,
I'm wrong to think she wanted any part of my life.
She probably just wanted hers back,
the way she remembered it:
the wheatfields scratching at her calves,
the cranes murmuring above
in grey undulating mists
the blue sea asking her to come closer
her hands reaching for another.
Maybe all she wanted was to feel.

There is no age for that.

wholly creatures

Far be it from me to ask
for you to nourish my bones
past the age of 14.
That's my second and final age
where I get to build my own house
from the scars I carry like coins
(I dig for them, they are my currency).

Far be it from me to ask
for you to wait as I punish myself
exhaust myself
while I build this house, this stupid house,
the house that I hate,
and why should you wait
while my anger keeps me up at night
finishing it.

Far be it from me to ask
for you to give me a key
to the house, that stupid angry house,
that I built myself with stones and tears
and blood and years
the key is mine to find,
underneath blankets of fears.

Far be it from me to ask
that you make me whole,
for the only holy creature that exists

in this rotten paradise
is the one that I built myself,
from bones and blood and hair and sound,
not the stupid house that I just burned to the ground.

futures

Don't build me idols
when so many of mine leave.
Stone crumbles eventually,
and we're left with the plans
to the original design, fluttering in our hands
as the breeze of time rushes past.

Don't build me idols
when you haven't asked me if I wanted any.

Don't build me idols
when we don't have time to worship at their feet,
begging for them not to fail us.

Don't build me idols
when I stand here,
disappointed with your choices.

Don't build me idols
when I can make my own
with my blood, my tears,
my hands full of stone.
I'll create a world of glass and steel,
light and dark,
love and loss,
and I'll make sure the music that plays,
is my children's voices,
their future,

and theirs alone.
hiding

What do you want from me? *I asked*
Everything you're not prepared to give, *grief replied*
So I boarded up my heart against the wind—
the nails in my hands pierced the cage
as it grew smaller and smaller,
fleshy, empty,
my bones moved around it, protecting it,
like a dance.
I didn't stand a chance.
I turned the light off in my eyes,
the curtain of my hair
hiding me from the world.
Little girl, grief said.
Little girl.

why is it that people cock their head when they feel bad for you? Are they trying to understand you? Are they thinking about their own sadness? Are they planning their next sandwich or how much money they need to pay the neighbour that lent them money for cigarettes? Are they figuring a way out of a conversation that they don't want to have about the fact that you want to murder the crows that keep hovering over the grave that they just dug for the person you loved? Do they know how it feels, or are they trying to know how it feels, when all you can feel is a wet face from crying, and you can't even put moisturizer on your face because it slips off right along with that expensive eyeshadow that you shouldn't have bought but you did because you wanted to look nice for someone who can't even see you because they're dead? I should feel bad for them because I can't explain how I feel and when I try to I sound like an angry asshole standing next to a priest trying to read a prayer but all you want to do is cry and tell people how unfair it is that the person you love so much broke your heart by leaving. Dying is leaving, it's cheating on someone because you leave to go somewhere that has no pain and you leave the person standing there holding the pain right in their very bones and they can't do anything with it but be angry that the priest keeps talking in that strange soft voice that's supposed to make you feel better. Well, it doesn't. Nothing does, apart from crying, and then there goes that mascara. And your nose leaks. And your hands shake. And you wait for the person you want most to hear you to really hear you, and actually crawl out of the ground and say something but they can't because they're dead and if they did, it would be a zombie movie.

but what then, now

A friend told me that
today is actually yesterday,
and also tomorrow,
and the now is then,
all piled in,
and so I asked, when, exactly,
am I supposed to let go?
never, she replied.
because everything is gone, which means nothing is.
and so I sat with your memories,
and had tea with them that morning,
because you never really left.

like that

the only book on loss
is the one you don't know how to write.
it doesn't exist until you kind of acknowledge
that it doesn't.
yeah, I know, that doesn't make any sense.
but hear me out.
the book doesn't write the first page
until the one you love
writes themselves out of your life
and you're left with empty pages
curling under the weight of your tears.
then, maybe months later,
you grab a *then*, and a *how*, and finally *do I do this.*
then you wait.
anger is here, you notice.
And you invite it to write a page.
(anger tends to write a lot of pages, actually)
you wait some more.
envy appears, envy confuses you.
take me, why not me, it writes.
It only needs a few words.
and then you wait.
months later, an *I*
and then a *miss*
and then a *you*
whispers.
you hear it, but you don't want to write it down.
so it steps out of the shadows,

and takes your hand
and moves
the pen.
slowly.

I miss you, you write.
Every page, one line.
Every page, forever.
And love opens the door,
and sits down next to you.
It's like that, it tells you.
Love is written like that.

the woods

I always thought woods were so quiet.
Too quiet.
But when I stood in the silence,
it's only when I closed my eyes
and felt comfortable in the darkness
did I hear birdsong.
Darkness magnifies
all the things you never notice.
Green trees with their snow-covered spines,
they move.
They creak and sing
when birds leave their nests,
the wind pushing them onward.
I move my head, my eyes still closed,
and I hear broken limbs
falling into the muffled loudness.
Another bird, calling to its mate.
A siren.
A chord of wind.
Ice melting off a piece of bark.
It's an uncovering that you witness
when your heart does the listening.

recipe

She never taught me
the right way to cook.
But her hands covered mine in flour
and her arms around me
taught me how things rise.

the days

It was Saturday but that doesn't mean anything
because Saturdays used to be about music
and laughter
and things that stung of hope.
My Saturdays would now have quiet roads,
and whining dogs,
and phone calls where things are taken away.
The stickiness of sadness
irritates me a lot.
It's never one day where you feel the same,
it's three days of sadness,
maybe a week of nothing at all,
and then two months of trying to catch my breath.
these aren't days, they're trials of time,
in the spaces between bone and skin within.

echoes

everything I never told you,
and none of the things I did,
was a life lived properly,
despite the days I hid—
from myself,
from the truth,
from love and pain
of seeing the children I'd lost, touching them again.

everything I never told you,
and most of the things I did,
were lies and half-truths about how to live.
I'm not ashamed of them,
it's not something I hold,
but I've given you these seeds
to grow, to discard, to wear like gold.

everything I always told you,
and what I didn't show,
was that loving you was the hardest thing
I'd ever know.

I didn't do it well enough,
and I hope you can forgive,
because the only way I can die in peace
is knowing that you carry my love,
and choose to live.

I never thought I'd see past my past, because my past had someone in it and now they're not here anymore, so why move ahead, right? Why not stop and stay still, and that way, nothing changes.

Oh, but everything always changes. That's life, they say. They say that a lot. *That's life.* We're all living for the lessons that dying gives us, right? We're all dying all the time.

One day, I won't exist.
Neither will you.
Neither will they.

All of us on a piece of parchment, waiting for our turn to slip down into the unknown, toes pointed down, arms above us, eyes shut, last breaths.

I stand at bridges, and the wind scoops under my shirt and the sleeves flutter and then rest again. Both sides of me at once: present and past. Feeling and felt.

I stand in a snowfall, hot pieces of snow hit my skin and melt into my hair. I think she might come back. That's the thing about magical thinking, you need it as entertainment, distraction, what a child does when they're hurt. It doesn't hurt, here's the shiny toy.

Come back to me. Just for a little while.
Come and walk through the door,
let me smell lilies ahead of your arrival.
Let me feel magic, just one more time.

my grandfather never knew me
like he did my mother
a blessing, really.
he sat with me,
my doughy arms around his neck,
and whispered fairy tales
that I would soon forget, but I do remember
his rough cheek against mine.
He was rough with my mother
but in a different way. Less loving.
And maybe anger comes from a place of love,
in some weird way.
Or a fear of loving too much, so much
that it makes you incapable
of wrapping your arms around the one person that you
need.
He loved me without fear,
but my mother felt invisible.

untitled

If you've ever sat up at 3am crying
because no one ever told you how hard this is,
if you've ever spent someone else's money
instead of your own, because they owed you for your
sadness,
if you've ever shouted at your children because you
blame them
for one of your babies being gone,
if you've ever stood at the edge of a cold sea,
or a busy road, and thought you might keep walking
because anything would feel better than what you're
carrying,
if you've ever held your child's hand but didn't feel it,
if you've ever told a lover you don't want them because
you were afraid of dying then I'll tell you that it gets
better.
You won't close those same doors,
you'll keep them open and let your sadness rush in like a
tidal wave,
breaking everything precious.
And one day you'll find yourself
sitting in the corner of that very empty room,
putting the pieces back together, slowly.
Slowly.

willing

I am willing to sit here
and share my story with you
and I find that it's an act of bravery.
because I will make you feel

     and hear

        and see

           and taste

              my pain

at the same time that I am.
I am willing to offer my heart like
an undelivered parcel
or a keepsake that you never want to break
you know the one that gathers dust
because you've left it on a shelf for too long.
Take me down, look at me.
You don't ignore your will when you need to eat,
so should you have a hunger, to open the door
and knock the dust off with your arms,
and look for what you need as the particles settle.
Be willing.
I'm here.
Find what you need (me to be, for you)
to find your way back (to me.

brother

There was an orchard
that sat in the sunrise

the girl sat under the pear tree
and watched her brother leave

the frost soon came and then the snow,
a dusting that danced and settled and hardened the
leaves.

the blackberries bled dark purple,
the pond became a mirror.

and she was still there. waiting.
there was nothing to eat but hope, nothing to drink but
memories.

that winter she starved
because his silhouette never again cut open the sky.

mora

suspended
like snow
like a thought
like the note ahead of a string waiting to play it
like rain waiting to fall
like lips yearning to kiss
like the waves waiting to break
like the storm waiting to descend in a crash
like the breath held right before bad news
like the world when it waits
and laces fingers
and prays
for joy.

and breathe again.

heavyweights

I don't know if I ever told you
that he shouted at me
screamed like an angry sea
when I asked him to love you three.
He told me to give up,
give in,
admit that it was sin because my body
was like an angel's: fallen.
I took his voice as a kind of love,
knocked out with a fist in a soft leather glove,
maybe I deserved it.
Maybe I didn't earn
the kind of affection that could persuade
a change in direction.
So I stayed,
and was unafraid
of the scars he laid on my heart.
It was a start, at least,
to beg that love be a feast
but I was only allowed two.
Her, and you.
But never them. They were stolen from me,
so we could never fully be free.
But he always had
his hands, my scars,
and me.

atonement

Before I go, I need you to promise me forgiveness.
I couldn't close the door when she said that,
so I waited for the sirens to drive by before I spoke.
When, I asked.
And then the roses fell, their heads dying on the grass,
the blackberries, so sweet, turned sour
as if waiting for that hour,
and the vines thrashed and cut me and I bled,
And when I cried out, the piles of blackbirds on the fence
thrashed their wings and fled.
When I am dead, is what she said.

I don't need wooden crosses bearing witness to your losses.
That's not forgiveness.
I nodded my head. But I wanted to scream instead.

Forgiveness is rage and inky black
it's the poetry of silence when you kneel in a stream
waiting to be seen and be taken back.
It's begging the memories to fade when they are the memories
you want to evade. But you stay, and you watch them
unfold like whip marks on your skin, and you begin
to understand that forgiveness is the undoing of who I am,
who you are,
who we were, because forgiveness
is to be disturbed, held, and rattled in its cage
and written down with tears on a page
on those days when you profess to hate me most.
Your grief sings in anger and protest

and plays with perfection as a badge
that I never had. And so, you have to let me go.
Forgiveness is opening your hand without mine there to touch.

I closed the door, my sadness coated the floor.
But when I opened my palm,
a blackbird rested there,
and then came the dawn.

finding you/myself

I lost my mother once,
when I was 5.
I let her hand go when I wasn't supposed to,
and I walked away straight into a wide world,
the sky was bright blue, and I felt so small,
the buildings were so dark and tall.

I lost my mother again when I was 17,
I let her hand go because I was supposed to,
according to my group of friends. They knew
I was old enough to stand on my own,
even though I didn't feel fully grown.
No one ever does, I guess.

I lost my mother again when I was 32,
when I became a mother too.
I replaced her hand with a tiny one it seemed,
and time sped by in a feverdream
of nights that bled into days,
of endless thoughts and sticky days.
I lost my mother suddenly when I was 65,
she let my hand go, hers grew cold and mine still alive
with love, desperate to crawl back in her arms,
and retreat into the recesses of when I was 5.
I begged for her to come back,
to look for me like she used to, when I was small,
when the bright blue world swallowed me up,
and the buildings were so dark and tall.

growth

This is empty, I said
when you handed me the wooden box
etched with stories from so many years
the grooves bored through
almost to the middle.
Worn, tired, paths.
Look inside, you told me,
and I waited years before I did. I hid.
I waited for something to appear inside,
for the tangled thing inside me to undo, but it never did.
This is empty, I said again.
You pressed the box to my heart, closed like a fist, and
said
so is this.
So I lifted the latch, pried the old wood open to see,
and it was me.
I was hollow, carved out, emptied and discarded
grief had stolen everything and left shards of hope
and departed.
And then I saw,
a little piece of me, and grew a tree.
Roots don't need evidence of hope,
they just need constant care and love to exist,
to be.

It's not that it has nowhere to go, actually, because it goes everywhere:

it's in the coffee that I make that I know you'd love but then I ruin it with too much sugar, it's in the baby clothes that I fold that you'll never wear again because you never lived long enough to drop pasta sauce on them, it's that song that plays on the radio that I have to shut off because that's the one where you promised me forever but you left, it's the drawer that still has your perfume in it (the one I bought you that one time for Christmas that you pretended to love but didn't), it's the questions I ask out loud to an empty room hoping you might answer them, it's the dog-eared recipe in the Joy of Cooking that you always used to make when I'd come in from the cold, it's the cigarettes that my lungs soak up in the hopes that I'll hear you scold me, it's when the glass that you used for cognac slips out of my hand and shatters into a million sparkling fragments and I know I can't save them all but I still want to. Desperately want to. Grief goes everywhere. It spills everywhere.

conversations, part 1 (of infinite)

'There's no mystery though,' you said to me. 'It just *is*.
We all carry that with us, the *knowing*.'

My coffee sat untouched, the fluorescent light on the
ceiling giving it a grey tinge. 'The knowing,' I repeated.

'Yes.'

I stirred my coffee with my pinky, letting the liquid drip
onto the white table. 'See, the knowing is problematic.'

'Why?'

'Because the only thing I know is that one day, I'll have
to brace myself, clutch at the table and get ready for that
pain, that lightning, to shoot straight through my insides.
I have to *take* it. That's the knowing. The knowing that
I'm living with someone who I'll lose one day. The
knowing that I'll have to adjust who I am, to that. The
knowing that I'll want to replace that person, or thing,
with something else, but that it'll never be enough: not
enough love, or sex, or money, or wine, or cigarettes,
or—' I looked at the brown stain, not yet dried. '—
coffee. That knowing, it rots my insides. Makes me feel
hollow and heavy all at once.'

Your face darkened. 'So, no mystery then? You'd rather
know?'

'No, I'd rather not have to talk about this at all, and live in the world I imagined as a girl: forever, forever in love and never hurting.'

'But how would you ever know it was worth it, without losing it?'

'But is something only worth anything once it's lost?'

And neither of us knew the answer to that, so we sat in the harsh light of knowing the truth.

what my 11 year old said when I was crying that day

Did you know that even vampires
need to be invited into a house
before they can overpower you?
Love too, I think.
Love needs a reason.
But the thing with people dying, I'm pretty sure this is
what I read:
death just shows up with a fork and knife,
demanding to be fed.

advice

Get dressed, he whispered to me. He was standing by the
bed and the yellow sun was too bright behind his dark
silhouette.

So I pulled the blanket up and over my face.
'No,' I sighed. 'Not today.'

Why, he asked.

'Because I want the world to go away.' I pressed my eyes
tight against the tears that were stinging, lying in wait to
race down my cheeks.

You can't hide forever, he said.
The sun grieves leaving the moon,
but she rises just the same; her heart (day)breaks too.

When I reached my hand out for help,
he was gone.
and so were you.

a year of befores and afters

All in the garden, the first hot, sunny day of the year.
April. The trees surrounded us like leafy statues
still and quiet apart from the wind sweeping around
them. Color and sound. An imprint on my brain
like a scar on parchment.

I was alone, cold gravel under my feet
as I walked the dog,
pulling on his lead

peonies, I wanted peonies again,
I wanted the hot smell of fresh flowers
grieving deserves flowers

I imagine that it was a dream, that they lied in
that phone call that *she's gone, she died*
and then months of denial
many months many months

Month 1

I don't remember eating much because
I was drinking more than normal
whatever normal meant but
what does normal mean when
someone just disappears, vanishes and then
again, my children ask me questions I can't answer
when I just want to sleep. But sleep doesn't come

like a package deal with grief.
So, I weep, instead. And sit on my bed.

Month 2

Minutes began to feel like years felt like seconds
I woke up every day feeling like it was the day before,
I painted my lips and wore clothes
I'd never worn before.
Darling, I'd hear her in my dreams.
Darling there's no point in any of this
I'd laugh and cry at the same time
like some kind of terrible bliss
of knowing that she was right:
There was no light, no point, no fight
left in me.

Month 3

If I were religious, this would be the month
that I kneel and beg a benign disinterested man
to heal my scars, like the very same scars
he burned into the night sky;
he made them glitter and burn
so I wonder when it would be my turn.
I want to feel that heat, that spark,
I want to feel anything at all.

Month 4

Spring isn't the season for death, surely

and neither is summer, it's too painful
to see the regrowth and the evolution
when all you want to do is hide and seek
the absolution and forgiveness for something
you don't understand.
winter is the season for grief,
the snow lands and every time I walk familiar paths
I stamp it down, ready for another layer.

Month 5

I hiked a lot to remind me of the weight of you.
I didn't pack anything in it, because
an empty bag still has heaviness to it.
It's the hint of pressure,
the shell ready for something
to carry, to bring with me to another place,
I brace myself for it to fill again, and I wonder
where I'll be then, when I have to carry you again.

Month 6

When you love something, and let it go,
it comes back to you, you tell me.
But I loved you, I let you go,
and now I'm waiting. Come back
Tell me where to wait, so I can see
your silhouette, like a blackbird against the snow,
coming back to me.

Month 7

Days turn into nights turn into
days and nightmares and daydreams
of endless memories that shift like watercolors
on dry blank slates. I drink more, and sometimes
less, depending on who's watching me.
My heart feels like a stone in the sea.
I hear voices ask me do join in with games
and watch television and fix their knees
grazed with play
but I move through moments with a fixed gaze.
I try and see signs too, I never believed in them
before you.

Month 8

Nothing is constant, and therefore everything is.
If everything is urgent, nothing is.
I stand on a constantly shifting middle ground,
my feet don't straddle absolutes anymore,
because that's not where you are, or where grief lives.
Broken things never settle in one place.

Month 9

The monotony of hope!
the monotony, you remind me.
hope, though! I shout.
I force myself to believe it
because no one else will try and convince me.

they all dip their heads to the side when I tell them you
died.
I keep shouting.
I do it to keep myself alive.

Month 10

Christmas bells ring out
it was your favorite, always
like a glittering winter in your heart
old secrets buried deep
thousands of miles ahead of you that you always keep.
or maybe, it's the hope of spring.
Maybe that's what you wanted,
A chance to do it again,
the way you'd hoped to, when people told you to give
up, and give in.

Month 11

I've learned to let you go,
without feeling that stone of guilt in my belly,
without feeling my breath ragged
without crying so loudly that birds fly in jagged
lines across the sky.
I've learned that you'll stand next to me
in the moments where I've set you free.
I've learned that pain exists, warm within,,
under blankets and shields of joy,
right in the bones beneath happy skin.

One year

Colors explode and fight through the earth, spring brings
an explosion of light and sound, birdsong so irritating,
but the sound tells me
that I have no choice but to loosen my grip on the last bit
of snow,
and the last memories of your voice slowly withdrawing,
melting through my fingers, the coldness finally thawing.

mundanity

The garbage men do their job
even though you died.
They empty the glossy green bins
morning sun shining on decay
and yet how rude that they forget
that my pain is still here, rotting away.

The leaf blowers create a wall of noise
cleaning up the wild mess in happy gardens,
stepping over my tired body,
vines threading through my hair,
as I lay staring at the sky
wondering why.

The postman wears blue,
every day, just like I do.
But his arms are always full of news
for expectant others
and my hands hold nothing but questions,
and I wish I could write answers to you.

I suffocate the orange in my hand,
my nails piercing its skin.
They asked me for juice, they asked me
to make them a bright little breakfast, bright happy
children.
But all I do is want someone to dig their nails in me,
slowly,

so I can feel something sink in.
what you told me about grief and books

Spend some time thinking about the ending—
love lives in the knowing of endings,
but don't allow yourself to search for it.
It comes quietly,
one day, as you wait for the bus
and you hold it in your warm hands,
you're comforted by the knowledge
that it's there, but that you can delay
seeing the words
until you have no choice
but to turn the page.
and the next chapter begins with
the next day.

color in the afterdays

The morning after I died,
they uncovered me.
They washed my face with soft flannel,
and brushed my white hair with an alabaster comb.
They painted my nails in a slick red sheen,
dressed me in emerald silks and ran their hands over my body
to press my skin, to make me clean.
The air became sweet and cold,
and I remembered a dream that I had
when I was a girl—
A dream where the stars
dressed the world like silver diamonds,
facets scattered and waiting to cover us at night,
and that only in death,
would I be ready to discover
that my old, tired lips
would forever be softened, shining like gold,
with promises of love from another.

You think a lot about death, really.
You feel sorry for yourself and you
drink a little, and then sometimes a lot,
and then you take out old photographs
and shuffle them like cards and gamble on which version
of them will
make you cry the hardest.
And then you invent stories in your head
about who they were,
and you write them down, drunk, elated, worshipping.
You get distracted,
because the words look stupid and weak,
and then sometimes they look too evocative, too bleak.
You open old paint tins
and try to imagine their face
but you sitting there painting seems out of place.
So you try and play music that they hated
and you look at the letters they wrote,
the sweaters they knitted,
the poetry they created.
You walk down the road to visit
the gardens they grew,
and talk to the people they knew.
You watch old movies that remind you of them
(well not really them, but maybe
the idea of who they could've been),
You walk without even knowing where you are
or why you're there.

And you think about the dying, not the death,
and how the dying felt
and if they saw more of the life they'd hoped to,
and if you'd done enough for them,
and you try to stop thinking about yourself so much,
in order to write some words about the life they'd
actually lived
and then you sit, in silence
and try and stop the words
from bleeding under your tears.
And then you think about life,
and how you're grateful for it,
and that they lived. Truly lived their life.
And so you begin to write.

symphonies

The quiet before,
like a held breath, while the strings tighten.
The cold metal, gold brass tightens.
Arms held up, as if feeling the rain,
the strains of hope and sadness fighting each other.

Fingers gently on the right keys
the ones that sound sharp and wild,
the ones that remind you to curl up and hide
from the things that you fear most.
Fingers gently on the wrong keys, then,
the ones that teach you to hesitate
the discords heavy in your ears
the years of practice and practice
bracing for new sounds to surround you.

Fingers gently,
gently. You have to sit down and be ready
for empty pages, for the echoes off the walls,
you have to be waiting for it all.
Held breath.
Wait..

And then it begins.

magical sorrows

A friend of mine
used to buy flowers for herself
on the anniversary of her lover's death.
She would water them from her teacup,
and carry them in her pocket in the storms,
still singing under the willow trees,
worshipping their sad little leaves,
her voice cracking with the thunder. Bereft.
I would laugh at how strange this behaviour was
until the morning you left.

pretending

As though it were
a normal day
where I wrapped my hands around a glass
and tried not to crush it
simply for its empty beauty.
It's faultless, but the reminder
stabs my heart every time I see it.
So I want to destroy it,
my teeth ache when I pretend to cherish its fragility.

It feels comfortable
to despair here
for a little while,
like standing in the middle of a wave,
the push and pull of the sea around you,
that's grief too.
It feels comfortable to allow myself
to stand here.
Despair doesn't have to be a four-choir tragedy.
Sometimes it whispers behind a softer mask.
It sits next to me, asks me for my time,
makes me feel like my task
is to matter in that moment.

all I want to say is

I miss you.
I love you.
Come home to me,
I will slip the latch off the doors
and slide the windows open
It will be ice cold, some days,
the ice encasing the trees.
But the clouds will lace around your memory,
bring them to me,
and set us free.

desert travelling

You are my country.
You are my history—
dusty trails and animal entrails
and thin trees with split limbs like needles,
dry and exposed.
And I keep walking.
The trick I think is to love,
like a blindness.
A mother doesn't love her own child
out of kindness,
it's a promise to love as a kind of violence,
Viciously adoring the acrid beauty that's around.
Oh, what I wouldn't give
to find you again,
so I can find my place,
know my own ground.

midnight circus

You knocked softly that day,
I didn't hear you arrive, your footsteps like young paws
in the snow.

Hello.

You smiled, and tried to open the door.
You waited for me to be ready
It was the soft relief of you in the mottled glass
that made me want to know more.

Where are we going, I wondered, and I was timid, so I
closed my eyes.

Somewhere unexpected, you replied.
You can't choose. And don't wear shoes.

Why, I replied.

Because you'll need to know where you are, in a night without stars.

And we walked as the sun bled
its orange into the grey.
I saw the old dog walker and he smiled
as if he knew.
I think he knew, that day.
I passed the store
where you used to buy those bread rolls,

the warm white ones with salted tops we used to tear
apart with our hands
and dip into sweet butter.
We always learned that way,
with feeling and taste,
with each other.

You were ahead of me now, waiting. The door opened
like it was cut out of the world
(the world felt thick and black)
and then you told me to climb
the cold steel rungs of the ladder,
without looking back, but also never too far,
up to the top where all I could see
was an absence of stars.
No color or shape, just a thin rope like a scar,
for me to walk across,
stretched tight across the night.

Walk ahead, you told me, like it was a test.
It's the only way to see the rest.

So I toed the line, tenderly, swaying to one side and then
the other, and sometimes balancing all of me down the
middle, like I'd known how
all along. Like an old song.

In all honesty, I rarely sing anymore, but this time,
just this time, it felt good, where I stood.
So then I held my breath and
tightened my chest, set my teeth,

and finished the rest,
I saw that the other side had nothing
but another ladder down, hard and cold.

You told me there was more, I said, as my feet slipped.
There is, but you have to get to the bottom.

I didn't enjoy that bit.

I touched the ground without making any sound
(sadness needs a kind of quiet around),
I saw the fire eater in gold skirts and red paint circling
her eyes, devouring the licking flame and putting it out
inside.
Smoke ran like capillary rivers out of her mouth.
I wanted to feel how it burned, I wanted to feel my story
turn, I wondered if the meat inside me,
that had corroded by now,
would melt or spark or turn to dust,
I wanted answers to my *why* and my *how*,
but maybe there was nothing left by now.

My face was glazed with salted tears, so I turned and saw
the magician cutting himself in two and making himself
disappear.

I saw the dancing girls in gilded skirts and the acidic
smiles of energetic clowns, and I fell backwards into their
arms and let them pour mouthfuls of spirit down my
throat as if I wanted to drown.
I wanted to watch the world

from a quiet sunken place,
I really did.
You saw me give up,
and I saw you walk over to me,
So I turned and ran and hid.

And then the lion tamer found me,
and strode over smelling of leather and oil and his hand
tore at me and he gave me the whip
but I broke it in half and instead I pried open the lion's
jaws like I'd somehow
wanted it to laugh, and I crept in,
curling up in the wet heat of its roar and I wondered if
any of this would ever end.

I wanted you back,
I wanted just one day, one more.
And I wondered if my heart
could bear to be entertained
with so much sadness anymore.

Listen, you said, and you pulled me out, teeth-scars
grazing my arms,
my heart,
my ribs,
my calves.
I can't listen anymore. Take what you came for.

And the settling gold dust hovered quietly,
and the desperate shouts for more,
and the flying tenderwalkers

and the puzzle of bodies
with their feet pressed in the soil keeping score,
and the severing of parts only to put them back
in new places,
and the painted laughing faces,
and the fire and white-hot flames and the
shining girls as they cry and twirl
perched on breakable stages
in front of a dying world,
and the crust of sweetness on the rotting apples,
the way they bury their hope in the soil
to grow new mothering trees,
and hopeless vengeful seas,
and the elation and despair and shock
as they all swallow their fear and clasp hands,
these witnesses, this crowd—
you took her hand, as she was sleeping,
and you left me there, drowning in my tears, weeping,
watching it all tangled in a beautiful shroud.
And you told me,
grief lives here, in this tragic terrible beauty,
and it will always be loud.

the switch

Here's the contract:
first there's you.
And then there's us.
And the *us* spends time
learning from *you.*
And it's always the normal things—
like the right temperature for tea
or the best fit for gloves,
or the stupid ways we talk about
how we fell in love.
And then over time,
the *us* becomes *me*
because once you go,
I can't leave.
I have to stay
and sit with your ghost and drink cold tea,
and return the third pair of gloves I bought
because they never fit me.
Like you did.
And now there's a space here
a cavern here
an empty room here
without *us*, without *you* knocking to enter,
a doorframe without a center.
And every time I walk through,
I realize that the contract I signed
was the one everyone has to,
right at birth, right at the lightest bit:

they leave
so you can walk through the door
without their shadow blocking it.

the bargain

What's my prize, I ask you.
What's my forever?
You promised me something like it
and now my arms are empty,
and my mind races like clouds
skipping across the grey skies
racing from the storm.
I've given you hope, you whisper to me.
I laugh. Hope isn't what I asked for.
You close your eyes and say, *but it's what you need.*
And my arms were suddenly heavy with all of it;
the heirlooms,
the stories,
the dismantled typewriters
no longer irritating me
with stories that I never knew
about you.
My arms dripped with runner bean stalks
and grass stained palms
and spilled wine staining the walls
and I knelt under the weight of it all.
I asked you for relief, but you added more.
You added a lifetime of open windows
and closed car doors
all so much louder than the days before.
You added songs she would never sing again,

clothes that hung from her arms as she grew thin
the last days where I felt her bones
beneath my touch.
There are countries she'd never seen,
but do I take her there and imagine that she'd been?
That's the gift, you tell me.
You traded her for a new story a new life.
And this, I realized, is my gift.
It's how I bring her back.
This is why I write.

In order to lose things,
we have to open other things:
the losses are a result and a cause
of the things we need in that moment.
Like a room suffocating from heat,
or humidity,
or cold.
We open the window to let it all out
but in doing so,
we invite relief in.
When I lost you,
I opened myself to it all
and forced myself
to be grateful for it
because those spaces
are the lessons.

as you left

the conversation always leaves a question,
a cup of tea half drunk
the tone of a question, hanging in the air,
a sigh,
a pause,
the watch that needs winding,
the stuck kitchen drawers
everything contains answers
within the silence or the desperation
to open what's inside.
Every day, I tried.
I tried to understand
why this was mine.
You left me time.
And once I realized that the line I needed to cross
was the one where anger ran against patience,
and lost,
I learned that love and pain
sit pleasantly beside each other,
their faces turned up to the heavens,
swallowing the rain.

things are alive here

you said to me
as I watched you set fire to empty boxes,
the same ones that you'd carried on your back
hoping to set them down somewhere,
anywhere,
the insides spilling out
as your hands reached into me for light.
You wanted answers
after you'd travelled around the sun
like a lonely tourist
taking in all that warmth,
paying for it with adoration.
It killed you.
So you carried whatever you had left
and asked me to help you burn it
to worship what you'd lost.
I had light,
you had darkness.
There was killing
and creation,
and the planets kept spinning in spite of you
with their starlight pouring out of ancient wounds
and you find what you need
suddenly
and you seduce that will, that fight
you take it all in your arms—
every broken bit
and you set it all alight.

At a certain age, the light that you live in is inhabited by the shades…I'm very conscious that people dear to me are alive in my imagination…These people are with me. It's just a stage of your life when the death of people doesn't banish them out of your consciousness, They're part of the light in your head.

Seamus Heaney

etyana Denford is a Ukrainian-American historical
:tion author, writer, and translator. Her first novel,
otherland, was longlisted for the Reader's Digest
:lf-Published Book Awards and has been published
obally to critical acclaim. Her writing has been
iblished on Elle.com, Vogue, Medium, and she also
)sts The Craft and Business of Books on YouTube, all
)out how to navigate the creative process of writing a
)ok and how to better understand the publishing
dustry. She currently lives in New York with her
isband and three children.

www.tetyanadenford.com
@tetyanawrites

Printed in Great Britain
by Amazon